Mat's Big Day

Written by Antony Lishak

Illustrated by Mike Phillips

Auntie Sharon

had a surprise for Matt.

She was getting married...

and wanted Matt
to be the pageboy.

Matt did not know
what a pageboy was.

Auntie Sharon showed him a book about pageboys.

She showed him the special clothes.

The shoes were very shiny.

She showed him the church.
The church was very big.

She showed him the ring.

The ring was very shiny.

Matt showed everyone
he was a good pageboy.

It really was Matt's big day.